TO MY MOTHER, IN GRATITUDE

HARSHITHA NADIKUDA

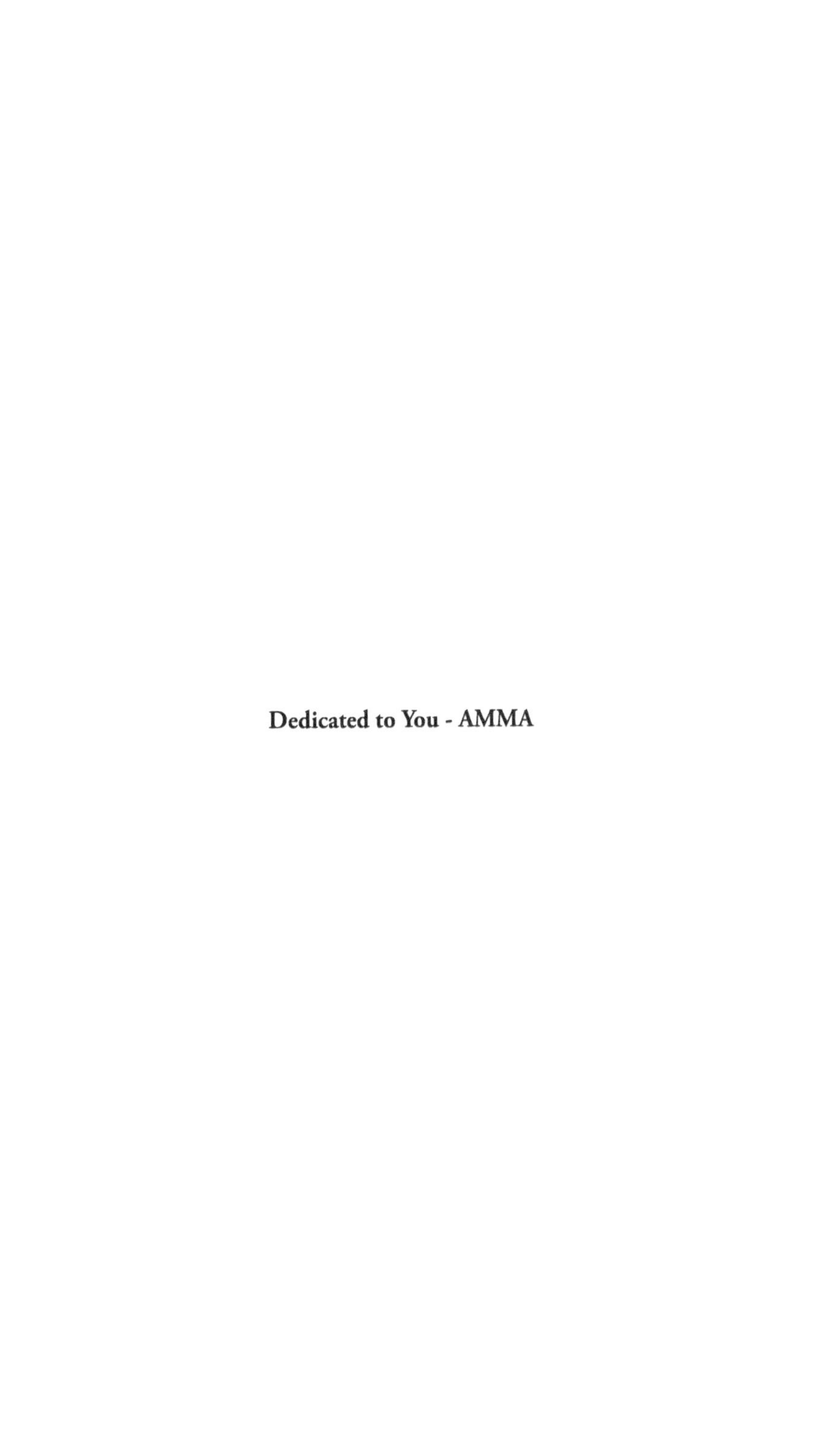

Dedicated to You - AMMA

Contents

Contents

Preface

"To My Mother, In Gratitude" is a collection of poems dedicated to Mother.

Mother is the most important woman in everyone's life. A mother sacrifices her happiness for her child. No one else can care for their kids the way a mother does. Mother's love is undefined!

Acknowledgements

I feel a deep sense of gratitude to God for guiding me in my every move.

My kind regards to my family, mentors and friends, who genuinely encouraged, supported and inspired me.

1. Mother- Love, Hope and Magic

Dearest Mother,
You are the one, and only one
Who shall never stop
Showering love on me.
If I could write a story,
It'd be the greatest ever told,
Because it'd be about thee;
For thy have a heart of gold.

Chapter2

Beloved Mother,

You're are an expert in mother's craft;

You mean a lot to me!

There are no similes and metaphors I could find

To compare thy and thee love.

Aren't you tired of teaching life lessons

Continuously?

Even though, you're a tiger mother

I admire you the most

For thou guides in every aspect.

Love for thee is colossal

Hate, not even itsy-bitsy;

I'd never keep mum

To say about you;

You gave memories of galore

By holding my hand every moment.

Chapter3

Magic, you do, indeed

Only you could do

Timeless, thy love

Hallucinates all my problems;

Euphoria presents thy

Reincarnation of I, would also be thee daughter only.

4. I do love!

Beloved,
Heart warming words of yours
Adore I;
Never ending care,
Unconditional love of yours, I do love!
Selfless love
Reallocating on me
Enduringly,
Empatetically abiding me, I do admire for-keeps!

5. Mother's Love

The mother's love is precious
Can't be owned with wealth.
Herein has emotions
Holding endless love,
And sacrifices too...
Mother's Love is something special
Which no word could explain;
It glows with all the beauty
Who owned is lucky for sure!
The aforesaid love
Is a splendoured miracle
Could be done only by the mother.

Chapter6

Oh! Mom
You make the sunshine
Even on a cloudy day;
You kiss all the pain away,
When I'm sick.
Your tender voice vanishes all my fears
And thee hands wipes all my tears.
Honestly, you do care
Keeping me safe and secure;
You make flowers bloom in spring,
And it is you, who always fixes my broken wing.
You caresses in such a way that
I could need nothing;
You're the divine of mine!

Chapter7

Dear supporter,

You're the life of my success;

You've always been there

When I needed you the most.

Even at the time of quite wild world,

You've guided me through your life;

You're a soul, which I could never stop loving.

You do make my life complete,

You're the pillar of my life

Supports me,

And makes me strong

To move ahead, fearlessly.

Infact, I would be nothing

Without you, amma!

8. Sacrifice

Dear Mother, You've always been a giver
You hold a heart which is so kind and true;
I wonder every time
How'd you easily sacrifice anything for us?
You always provides us, the best,
Every need, you do fulfill,
In every pressure, you do protect
Without thinking about thee!
Thy love may be equal to stars count
Or beyond!

Chapter9

Dear special one,
You're my mentor,
Who always overwhelms the darkness
And helps me in designing my life
In a most appropriate way.
You're the gardener of wind-blown wild flowers;
For the years
You've been filling support and confidence in me.
Your lessons helped
In building my vision, goal, mission and objective.

Chapter10

Beloved mother,
You're always by my side
Made my life stable
Filled with lots of bliss.
Your love is a drug indeed,
For which, my want never ends.
You're are only one
Who'd never stop loving
And protecting me even in the deadliest stroms.
You eyes holds a love-light shining
And may be that makes you more beautiful!

Chapter11

The marvellous gift,
Received from God; It is you
Nothing I need more!

Chapter12

Even though, you're heart bleeds in pain,
Your heart is broken,
Your heart is on flame,
You always hide it. Why?
Having the deepest scars,
You always bless your fruit
With a nourished heart.
How's is this possible, amma?

Chapter 13

The moment I glimpse at thy,
The love I feel relaxes me,
Vanishes all my tiredness indeed.
Thee pours love from the four chambered heart,
Deducing euphoria.
The quality of time
That you spend with me and family;
The quality of thoughts that you've
For us, is more than enough
To envision the deepest love you have for us.

Chapter14

Mom! What fills the energy in you to do anything for us?

How could you manage to be a teacher, doctor, chief and etc?

From where do you get lots of patience?

Why do sacrifice everything for the sale of family?

Why do you pray only for us?

Aren't you bothered about youself?

Why?

Which magic exists in you?

How could you create miracles for us?

Being a poetess, I'm unable to find suitable metaphors. Why?

I owe to your love, how should I repay, mom?

Chapter15

Amma! The bond that I developed with you
Can never be severed;
I, an organism
Grown nine months inside you
After that, growing under your guidence.
You carried me' nonetheless suffering pains,
Sharing your sustenance with me
Through your umbilical cord.
You nurtured me, a lot
Enduringly I do love you!

Chapter16

My brain hold the memories with you

Like the origami cranes

Hides them in hippocampus, dear mom.

You're my love, the love I ever need

Memories you gave since my birth, I adore

And please don't stop loving me abundantly for-keeps.

You dwell in my heart

And moments with thee resides in my mind;

For thee always endears my heart!

Chapter 17

Amma, you're the light
Even in the darkest night;
You're the shining star
That protects me in every war.
Tenderness on me, showers you,
Is the sweetest one;
The modesty
Is the abundant in thee.
I've nothing to fear,
When you're here,
Thy hand
Afterall, is my magic wand.

18. Lessons

With you by my side,
I can't go astray;
Never I'd go wrong, I beieve
For thy lessons accompanying me.

19. Don't you know this, Amma?

Amma, don't you know
To take care of yourself
To take a leave from household chores
To take rest when you're sick
To think about yourself?
You only know know how to love me and our family
I urge you, not to forget yourself in a journey of serving us;
We also do love you,
You are the apple of eye,
We want you to be happy, amma!

Chapter20

You,
Do love,
Fights with dark,
Produces bliss
Enduringly, though
Unrecognised
Thy glory;
My hero–
You!

21. A plea to forgive me

To my dear, with gratitude
I feel sorry!
I sincerely apologise
For all the hard times I put you in,
I mean my sorry, I swear;
I really do love thy,
I'll try hard
To make you happy.
It's my deepest apology
And a plea to forgive all my mistakes.
Never was and will be my intention to commit mistakes
Some of them happened accidentally
And I'd never dare to repeat, I promise!
Your soul, sole is the dearest of mine
I'm blessed to have you
I'd definitely make you proud.
Write I, words from my heart amma!
I LOVE YOU!

22. Happy Birthday Amma

God gifted me you, my mother,

For not to bother

About anything

As you are my wing.

B'day comes once in a year

Enjoy the day; Here

Expressed I, the love I have for you,

And the love you've for us too...

I desire to write a lot

But there no words to allot

To describe thy grandeur, completely

Because you care us eternally.

God sent me

A gift, i.e thee

Whom I love whole-heartedly

And also dearly.

Once again, I wish you Happiest birthday day, my doll;

From deepest core of my heart, I say thy is my all in all!

Thank You

Thanks for choosing "TO MY MOTHER, WITH GRATITUDE"

• 23 •

www.ingramcontent.com/pod-product-compliance
Lightning Source LLC
Chambersburg PA
CBHW031640170726
47990CB00018B/1567